An Unbridled Cadence:

A Bluegrass WarrioHer

D1400291

Lindsay Gargotto, USAF Veteran

Dedicated to all my sisters. It took me many years to formulate these words, then to actually write them down. Finally, I am able to share with them with anyone who may find some want/need/desire to read them. This is all because of my sisters. Thank you for the bravery and hope you instill me every day. Never forget your resilience. A special thank you to my daughters' for always believing in me – you are both the reason I still rise, and more.

In Sisterhood,

Lindsay Gargotto, USAF Veteran

2

CONTENTS

Canaries Who Survive

I am a miner of everything
that is green;
where no canaries die.

I believe in stories,
of all kinds –
each one clean and fresh,
a blade of grass.
Pluck one blade,
you take a breath.

Leaving the Blue Valley

Down in the valley
Where the blue grass grows

I picked a color
and then
I was plucked.

The color did not matter.
They will shoot down any which way.

So I thought, Aim High.

****

My parents dropped me off
at the janky hotel
in the dark.
Only my suitcase left
leading my hips.

My roommate, doe-eyed
Kentucky girl,
talked just like me.
We passed a pint.

She was the last Kentucky girl
I ever saw
in mighty, mighty Air Force.

Learning to be a Nobody, a Trainee

"One good thing is someone does the thinking for you"~ from
Always, Norb

When I first joined the military I believed I found a solution to all of my life's problems at 20 years old; a respectable, honorable solution after years of struggle and shame. The first night at boot camp I was the last girl-woman to arrive. It was dark, late – I think around 2:00 am. I was brought to the overhang concrete slab that would become my new home the next 6 ½ weeks. It was humid; the air was silent in a different way than Kentucky. The thickness so deep, it pushed against me. A TI met me (not mine), immediately began speaking with starchy, quick words. I could not keep up – I was exhausted, in shock, possibly hung-over. I laughed. He screamed.

The beds were filled and the bays were covered in darkness. I found one bed left in Bay One close to the front door. I was the third bed down. I laid in the iron-frame twin bed with its smoldering wool blanket and listened to the sounds of 65 sleeping women-girls.

Two-three hours later we were made to dump all of our belongings onto our beds. 65 of us; 2 of them. My TI and her Chief inspected all of our personal things, while we tried not to cry. Their hands touched what was left of home. No more scents, no more "Last time I touched this I was here." Now everything belonged to them. My memories now belonged to them. They tossed our belongings like a drug raid.

My TI found pictures of my family. She taunted me with them, came less than inch from my face with her spittle speckling and sticking onto my cheeks, my lips, even in my eyes. She had a voice with leftover smoke stuck in her throat. I wouldn't see those pictures anymore, she charred. Because I was a nobody, a trainee.

Regulations

Under the sun
my tiny bones sweltered
on the popping black top.

My throat worked hard
to untangle the strings;
although
it appeared content in curling
to the commands on demand.

I had a voice once.
It did not have strings:
quick, brilliant, touching,
like glory

Now my voice drummed a cadence

left...your left...your left, right, leeeeft...

Taking the Country Outta the Girl

I know I am gold;
richer than butter
and easier too
the myth goes.

I know the flight
of my empty eyes.
They scare crows
into holes down deep.

I changed my voice
I lost my music
I lost my sound
losing respect for me.

Athena's Warriors

The earth sat grained
by the hands of women
only to be ate up greedily,
by bloodless men.
There is so much mystery to this world
civilized by battle.

Women hover, spinning their wings into gold.
They live to polish free souls.
They are Queens, an army of Amazons,
ready for battle, pledging to their one-breasted scar.

These women, our women, walk among us
in the brilliance of their intuition. We know
the designs of dignified life – we are
the lives of the living.

Branding Day

I've been issued my new skin –
me and 65 other women
corralled into a room
briefed until utterly dumb.

Herded
into rooms, pile after pile
of peroxide-infused materials
to find our natural fit.

We will become exotic moths –
Unique and universal, blended.
Green, brown, and blue are *brilliant* colors.

Blue Zone. PT Zone. BDU Zone.
Canteens, boots, covers,
blousing straps, undershirts.
And a rucksack to carry it all.

All uniform. All standard-issued.
Gear on – a moth behind glass.

Cinderella's Boots

~Thank you, Vonnegut
(Double Exposure Poem)

It is all about the pants

My pants have cargo pockets

It prevents morning rants

Strings to blouse my ankles like sockets

Next comes the shirt

My sleeves starched and straight

I wait for the one that flirts

My chevrons creased, perfects mates

With my eyes, my shoes are always a test

My boots shine, and almost glitter

One on the right, one on the left – deciding the best

waiting for my feet to hit the daily litter.

The Command

I was a field tent
to keep you safe little one

but now, I am U.S. Property.

*The military says, "If We wanted you to have a baby - We
would have issued you one."*

A woman first. An airman first. A human first.
There is no real order

Starched Threads

She irons me until I sizzle,
creases my joints into perfect lines.
I fly on her like a paper airplane.

She sprays me, saturates me,
with starch that crusts in crevices
because she irons again
until it is burnt into my every fiber.

We wear each other today.
Even in the heat; my starch,
her oil are the perfect mixture –
our skins now threaded.

Calling My Cadence

I am soldier, an airman, a sailor, a marine, a coaste –
Woman, Female in my boots and in my BDU's.

Even if I have not worn them in 10 years –
those blousing straps, dog tags,
stripes and ribbons - they are all still my skin.

I shed into a perfect woman in formation.

I marched in step   always
believing in those sounds, the thundering feet,
the gait in our voices, the stream of our swinging arms.

I can't remember every cadence but I remember each woman
by last name and lost homes.

I am a woman, a mother, a co-worker, a patient, a veteran.

I was meant to march   always
for life and liberty in the pursuit of happiness.

My feet still thunder.

Latrine Queens

Hair loss of 65 women
from tying our hair back
until our necks shined.

Stench of 65 women
from the San Antonio heat
melting our every pore.

Vanity of 65 women
salvaging our femininity
without traces.

Toothbrushes were a commodity,
an irreplaceable tool.
For cracks, crevices. Late nights.
We were Queens of Clean.

Pretzeled Hair

The twist of a bun
my fingers locked skillfully
in my hair, every day.
Until I had sores
red and pocked
all down my neck.

My fingers can dance
in my hair now
with my eyes closed.

Eyes of Steel

My arms are steel trains
trained
to run empty
and full into
the nights and days to
build
buildings

for us to sleep false winks of
sleep with our eyes steeled open.

Queen Bee

I watch women dream into nights
away from their mother.
All with eyes tucked tightly
inside the rubbed-out wool

heads laying blank
without pillows.

We are soldiers that heel our way through doors
with make-up faces all mudded-up
down our necks to stay warm
because our hair is a fistful
or less
than 3 inches of bulk.

Natural women march, kill, and cry
to save lives. We last *forever*.

A Smile From Home
November 20, 2000 – to my Mom, Patti Works
[unrevised]

Home is so far away,
a fragment in my mind.
A vision of your face
slips into my head
ready to find me.
Your smile says everything
will work out, words of support
soothe my doubt. Your thoughts,
movements, always genuine –
always graceful. My angel.

My shoulders are back,
my chin is up with you
on my side – I have no reason
to hide. You are my inspiration.
Your daily sacrifices make
my feet move every day.
I talk to you and I know you hear
even with the miles between us
our hearts still touch.

Women Who See At Night

Still face
lace-up eyes that
hold ancient dreams of dark
and light. Her mouth holding mine strong –
No tears.

Inside of Glass

Before the bushes were silent and nestled
outside protected from the shallowed-out
plains. They were smart bushes -
all sapped up for the winter.

The bushes looked like home,
a place now as abstract as tears. But I could
touch the wind as it rippled the earth,
the same earth of mothers and sons.

Before, I spoke to my brother's like looking into glass,
when our stomachs filled up the same.
But in those tired out bushes and my issued-out legs
my brothers' melted the glass into my nightmares
of this is who *they* were to be

My blood was not the first blood to soak
the bushes that choked my mouth closed.

Salted Songs

You cannot bleed me dry.
I am blood.
I salt my wounds.
I slap my skin when it itches.
I tobacco my skin when it stings.
I sing with remedies.

Leave me in the woods.
Leave me in the bushes.
Just leave me.
I am the salt of my sisters
who walked before me.

Moral Combat

One walk to the dining hall
on a deserted base for Thanksgiving.
Three Navy guys, one Air Force girl.
They had nothing to do.
They took an opportunity.
Who would tell.
Who would believe.
It was dark. No names,
no faces. Only muffled screams,
and barbaric grunts. And they left
the Air Force girl in the bushes.

She pulled her uniform back on,
the Texas stuck to her skin.
Crawled into a walk
back to her dorm, alone.
Told no one.

The Big Bad Wolf is real, *everywhere*.
I know how I bleed.
I know how my bones splinter.
I know what happens to mind, my heart
when a piece of me comes up missing.

Thank you brothers for fucking me up
to learn all this about me.

Necessity

I know a little bit about numbers.

I know what a 1,000 drinks feel like
trying to black out at night, on *that* holiday.
Don't call it an anniversary. Don't celebrate
the bloodshed of others, and mine.

I know what a 1,000 pills feel like
in being diagnosed, labeled
correctly, incorrectly in a world
that shoves us so full of medicine
that our thoughts become clumps of mud.
Our memories become the past, and
we remain sunk in our own steps forward.

I know what a 1,000 cuts feel like
reminding me my skin still breathes,
that it is mine and no one else's. Scars
are my markers, the lines of my evolution,
the places no one else will touch – inside or out.

I know what a 1,000 men feel like
a few I even loved, 2 I even married
and then divorced. Loss is natural in love.
It is easier that way.

I know what a 1,000 lives feel like
once I was a child, who was loved,
who knew nothing of the world, then
I became a teen who forced out. As a young adult
things were taken, and then I learned to take.
I became about surviving. Now, I am trying to learn
to be in-between surviving and living.

The Grass Bleeds Blue

I began from legends
of one-breasted women
who were taken in the night as babes
trained to be hawks and doves.

I was born in a place
where a factory demolished
a small town, a city with one zip code.
One hospital. One grocery. One high school.
An urban legend today.

I was born to a land
where the grass blooms and bleeds blue,
and the trees and winds speak four tongues.
Where lakes and rivers run
that never need rain, and our horses
are only top pedigree.

I am from women
who were new mother at 16,
who sit around tables drinking coffee
and smoking cigarettes, who craft
and sew and quilt and cook, who
take care of their men, who leave
their men, who bury their children,
who birth children at 15, 16, and 40.
I am from women who work in
factories, in flower shops. Are teachers,
accountants, and stay-at-home moms
who do it alone blind. I am from
women who slept in barracks, tents,
and floors with wool blankets.
Who wore boots with blousing straps
that ribbed our ankles purple.
I am from women who always,
always survive.
I am from both sides of the sun.

Women of the Wild

I ran into a moose once, 9 months pregnant while in Alaska.
My first full-term pregnancy, 22 years old: Active Duty Air Force.

I was walking into the hospital
around a dark corner. It was December.
It was always dark. I had no idea
they were there, a mother and calf –
bigger than horses,
things of mountain myths.
I was a solid mark for her.
I remember the briefing they gave us,
"mothers will kill without hesitation".
It was a narrow space between me and the baby.
The mother a few feet away.
She looked up, all eyes and head –
and charged me. No hesitation. All fight.
I screamed,
and went to my knees, cradling my baby.
We both had the same fear.

She stopped, only a foot or two away.
I could feel her grassy breath on top
of my head. I stayed with head down,
knees to the concrete, and she and her
baby walked away – together.

I kneeled on the concrete in the blackness
on my skinned knees murmuring
to my baby that I had saved our lives,
that I loved her. I would always protect her.
Even in Alaska, even from the wild.

But I am still not sure
which one of us
was the wild beast.

When Roses Rise

I hear the cadence calling
every morning. It pulls my breath out.
And something larger happens.

I rise.

Silence Protects No One
(Thank you Audre Lorde)

I was called to the ER
to do a portable x-ray
I heard the young mother's screams alone in the hallway
for a documentation process
and my job was to walk right past her

I made a promise to never be silent again when another human is in
pain.

I walked into the room
where on the table
with tubes, needles
tangled, with leads stuck
underneath lay
a baby boy
9-months old, no longer breathing.
With only his young mother
to scream,   cry
because his father was somewhere,
secret
facing his own death, possibly
while his only son
fell into his final sleep.

And I wondered
did ever see his son breathe?

I still hear her screams as a reminder.

Metamorphosis

We will never know the first one:
the first battlefield
the first blood-soaked soil
after the rib was pulled
or the ape became man and woman.

The Queen Ant brings life.
She is brilliant. She is a strategist.
She will know how to maintain
her reign, because she alone
breeds the competition.

No matter what class she is born-
if she wins, she will change.
Battle of the fittest female.
She transforms.
She will grow wings,
an accentuated abdomen, and
become fertile.
It is the fight for fertility;
not dominance
that the female worker ants dance
until death.

She brings all life.
She is everyone's mother.
She *will* hold her reign.
She *will* work until death.

Females
are precious as apples
and dirt.

Flying Death, Always

not a battlefield
two glass buildings
full of neck ties and suits
mothers fathers armed
with key boards computer
screens brief cases
swivel chairs   that creaked.
full of daughters and sons.

I saw the towers:
obstinate   pillaring,
next to each other
my good-bye trip
before enlisting

one year later
burnt steel   dust
blood covered the
ground

none of them

signed a contract to die
like I did.

the clean up site
glass & steel
on our soil. Terrorism.

we all watched.
screens screamed.
me, a newly wed couple
still in training.
How this happened –
no one could
speak.
blank monitors hummed
so loud   we forgot
patients in the rooms.

fifteen years later
I sit on a plane
free   civilian
I cannot help to think
I am flying death   still.

Pumping Guns

History says, man says, media says:
Women warriors are sallow myths and stones
History says, man says, media says:
Women's minds too fragile, inadequate
strategy too complex; not our nature.

History says, man says, media says:
our figures too hourly in uniform
Even in the Garden of Combat, tempting.

History says, man says, media says:
Why, we are women. Mothers – assumed.
We should be thrilled with hearth and home.

History says, man says, media says:
Our bodies deny strength, speed, endurance -
we are not cut for combat: just kitchens.

History says, man says, media says:
in the wild it is the mothers who
are most fierce. It is instinctive.
History says, man says, media says.
History says, woman says, nature says.

Y"our" America

We are not equal in y"our" America.
I live here, ignorant by circumstance
and smart by consequence.

Y"our" America is where babes
are stored in cardboard boxes,
and the parents eat their nails for dinner.
That is a good night.

And you can be white, and you can be poor,
you can be black, you can be a woman,
you can be gay. Any combination of these
leaves us all wanting, needing, dying.
This is how Ameri"can" defines us.
The bootstraps are strangling us all.

The War Always Comes Home

Her seeds extracted
and starved. Mornings and nights
collapse under her
red skirts where eyes hide
and the pain of death goes silent.

Flesh, Fire, & Rain
(For those in recovery)

I am a woman all flesh and bone.
I am a woman by birth and word.
 I make myself every day.

I am a veteran all commands and orders.
I am a veteran all sacrifice and love.
 I make myself every day.

For you brother, for you sister, for you country,
and all the lips I have never met
let my lips bring beauty to the nothing
and everything we stand for. I still march, crawl,
and elbow out the door every day.

I can still set a fire,
 even when I end up in rain.

In the Field

Poppies root war home
Field stripping our minds to death.
But can you blame a plant?

Restorative Hearts

Part I

I laid back
arms stretched
heart open waiting
for the breath of peace.

I work with hearts
every day
that beat against beat.

21 veterans commit suicide die a day.
Violence does not bring peace.

Fear, suffering, and shame
are the powder that fills [then shoots] the gun.

Part II

a restorative heart never stops beating
we are capable of infallible love

freedom is inside the god we trust
we are capable of indivisible love

We can lead a nation of restorative hearts.

American Satire

I am satire.
I am genius.

You can try
and pit me (against)
                    but I am deeper than blood.
Watch me dry
and never flake.

I can be death that is still alive,
or I can be woman

we both will never leave beauty.

Heartbeats are what I eat.

They sound me down
so that I can talk words
that you cannot break.

She Didn't Just Sacrifice *too*

Have you seen those women
spangled high on our flag?

They lead the light that makes
our sky roll to the earth every morning.

We served to make you safe.
We fly with everything to lose.
We are grandmothers, mothers, sisters, daughters -
who were told stay behind. That war was not for us.

Yet,
each of us, willingly, deploy our bodies
to bring us home, to bring you home.
We each fall in.

Women say to me:
"I want to be proud to be a veteran."
But experience is a bitch.
Silent truths are heavy,
especially the older they become.
Women have been warriors from the beginning
and we will be until the end.

Sisters, we are the home
for which it *still* stands
keeping the blue alive and dignified,
the white opening our sky free and high,
and the red written in truth and purity.

We are the Sisters of Revolution.

Resting Form
(Response to Tim O'Brien *The Things I Carry*)

The things I carry sit blank
where silence lays heavy
waiting to form deep in my throat,
sifting in the bowels of my mind.

These things are waiting
for me to theorize, therapize
this suffering into print,
a genius of myself true
and false. The ink stains my body.
Words.

There is never the right pen
to mark them as legible forms.

Or paper smooth enough
to soak their fibrous meanings.

Or the right color to stroke
their significance to life.

Or the right person to dance
in their shadows to form.

These are the things I carry –
words that catch my tongue
to the sun every morning
and the moon to lay them
to shadow them into the night.
There is rest for the silence
I still carry.

Morning Huntress

I keep shining without light.
I am the bruises
underneath your morning eyes.

I have already chewed
through the meat of my tongue.
I still have some shrewd dignity.

In this room, a veteran's earned
Temple of Insanity – I know these faces.
These voices. These warrior hearts
that beat down their own souls.
A drill done – time and time
again, but always with pride.

We have roads instead of lines
gunned into our hands. A warriors tattoo,
so we can march the world into step,
because we are the huntresses of truth.

The Land I Served

"All you write is what you see" ~ *Woodie Guthrie*

Before
I went walking that ribbon of highway
To now be cutting the uniform
that was once
my skin
into a postage-stamp size
or smaller scraps, put in a beater
And I saw below me that golden valley
made into a unique batch
of foaming pulp.
This land was made for you and me.

I added ingredients – we added
From the California to the New York Island
to our story; to place our story:
Hemp, sugar cane, tobacco.
To the sparkling sands of her diamond deserts

We started with moldy stalks –
A voice come chanting
Tobacco remnants, caked with time.
From *fields* once *waving.*
We cleaned them
until the brown
ran out. *And I followed footsteps.*

I poured the pulp into the tub
When the sun comes shining
took my screens,
and sloshed from side to side
as the fog was lifting
from the ocean that morning
I roamed and rambled
trying to perfect   imperfection
underneath trees that understood.

This land was made for you and me.

Taking my screen while
all around me, a voice was sounding
laying it on wet mats
levering just right – hoping
for each something that looked flat.
These motions repeated
I saw above me that endless skyway
as the tears rolled
into my tub, now a part of my paper.
This land is your land, this land is my land.

Our paper dries
When the sun comes shining
stuck to windows,
crimson and gray stained glass,
in racks, uniform flags hanging –
waiting to be filled with the
rest of the story.
And all around me, a voice was sounding

With this land,
with this uniform,
I followed footsteps
now conjoined forever

This land was made for you and me.

Made in the USA
Lexington, KY
13 September 2019